5-04

FRANCISCA ALVAREZ

THE ANGEL OF GOLIAD
EL ÁNGEL DE GOLIAD

TRACIE EGAN

TRADUCCIÓN AL ESPAÑOL:
EIDA DE LA VEGA

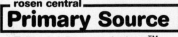
rosen central
Primary Source
Editorial Buenas Letras™

The Rosen Publishing Group, Inc., New York

Published in 2004 by The Rosen Publishing Group, Inc.
29 East 21st Street, New York, NY 10010

First Bilingual Edition 2004
First English Edition 2004

Cataloging Data

Egan, Tracie.
[Francisca Alvarez. Bilingual]
Francisca Alvarez, the Angel of Goliad / Tracie Egan; translation into Spanish Eida de la Vega.— 1st ed.
   p. cm. — (Primary Sources of famous people in American history)
Includes bibliographical references (p.   ) and index.
Summary: Profiles a Mexican woman who saved more than twenty Texan rebels taken prisoner during the Texas Revolution from being shot under General Santa Anna's orders.
ISBN 0-8239-4157-4 (library binding)
1. Alvarez, Francisca—Juvenile literature. 2. Goliad Massacre, Goliad, Tex., 1836— Juvenile literature. 3. Women heroes—Texas—Goliad—Biography—Juvenile literature.
4. Women—Mexico—Biography—Juvenile literature.
[1. Alvarez, Francisca. 2. Goliad Massacre, Goliad, Tex., 1836. 3. Women heroes. 4. Mexicans—Texas. 5. Women—Biography. 6. Texas—History—Revolution, 1835–1836.
7. Spanish language materials—Bilingual] I. Title: Francisca Alvarez. II. Title. III. Series.
F390.A35E35 2003
976.4'03—dc21

Manufactured in the United States of America

Photo credits: Cover, pp. 5 (bottom) Presidio La Bahía, Goliad, Texas, photos by Dallas Hoppestad; p. 5 (top), 27 courtesy of Mission Espíritu Santo, Goliad State Park, Texas Parks and Wildlife Department, photo by Dallas Hoppestad; pp. 7, 11 (top) Library of Congress Geography and Map Division; pp. 9, 13, 21, 23, 25 courtesy, Texas State Library and Archives Commission; p. 15 Broadsides Collection, Earl Vandale Collection, Center for American History, University of Texas at Austin; p. 17 Print Collection, Miriam and Ira D. Wallach Division of Art, Prints and Photographs, The New York Public Library, Astor, Lenox and Tilden Foundations; pp. 19, 29 Dallas Historical Society

Designer: Thomas Forget; Photo Researcher: Rebecca Anguin-Cohen

CONTENTS

CONTENIDO

1 WIFE OF CAPTAIN TELESFORO ALVAREZ

Francisca Alvarez was a Mexican woman who is remembered as an American hero. She saved the lives of more than 20 Texans in the Goliad Massacre. For this, she is known as the Angel of Goliad.

It is not known when or where in Mexico Francisca was born. Her family history and her childhood are also mysteries. At some point she was nicknamed Panchita.

---

1 ESPOSA DEL CAPITÁN TELESFORO ALVAREZ

Francisca Alvarez fue una mexicana considerada heroína en Estados Unidos. Ella ayudó a salvar las vidas de más de 20 texanos durante la Masacre de Goliad. Por este motivo, es conocida como el Ángel de Goliad.

No se sabe cuándo y en qué lugar de México nació Francisca. La historia de su familia y de su infancia también son un misterio. En algún momento empezaron a llamarle Panchita.

Above, a mural depicting the Goliad Massacre. Below, a painting of Mexican soldiers guarding American captives.

Arriba, un mural describe la Masacre de Goliad. Debajo, una pintura de los soldados mexicanos vigilando cautivos estadounidenses.

Sometime between 1834 and 1835, when she was thought to be in her late teens or early twenties, Francisca became a close companion of Captain Telesforo Alvarez. Francisca and Alvarez lived as a married couple. Although there is no record of a legal marriage, Francisca was known as Alvarez's wife.

Entre 1834 y 1835, cuando Francisca debía de tener alrededor de 20 años, se convirtió en la compañera del capitán Telesforo Alvarez. Francisca y Alvarez vivían como si estuvieran casados. Aunque no existe ningún registro de matrimonio legal, Francisca era conocida como la esposa de Alvarez.

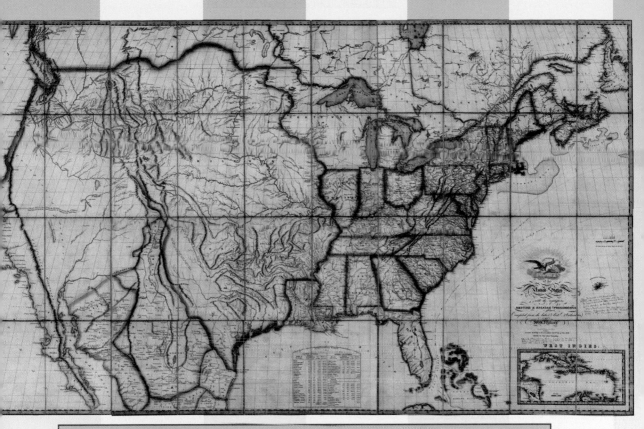

A map of the United States in 1816. As Americans moved westward, they coveted Mexican territories.

Mapa de Estados Unidos en 1816. A medida que los estadounidenses emigraban hacia el oeste, empezaron a codiciar los territorios mexicanos.

Captain Alvarez was a commander of Mexican forces during the Texas Revolution. Captain Alvarez was born around 1803. He was from the Mexican town of Toluca. His legitimate wife was Maria Agustina de Pozo. He abandoned her in 1834, leaving her with two small children.

El capitán Alvarez fue uno de los jefes de las fuerzas mexicanas durante la Revolución Texana. El capitán Alvarez nació alrededor de 1803. Era natural de la ciudad mexicana de Toluca. Su esposa legítima era María Agustina de Pozo a la que abandonó con dos hijos pequeños, en 1834.

The flag of the independent Republic of Texas (1839)

La bandera de la república independiente de Texas (1839)

Francisca followed Captain Alvarez around Mexico and southern Texas while he carried out his military assignments. They traveled through Copano Bay, Goliad, Victoria, and Matamoros. She gained a reputation for aiding Texan prisoners who were captured by the Mexican army.

Francisca siguió al capitán Alvarez por México y el sur de Texas mientras él cumplía con sus deberes militares. Viajaron por Copano Bay, Goliad, Victoria y Matamoros. Ella se hizo famosa por ayudar a los prisioneros texanos capturados por el ejército mexicano.

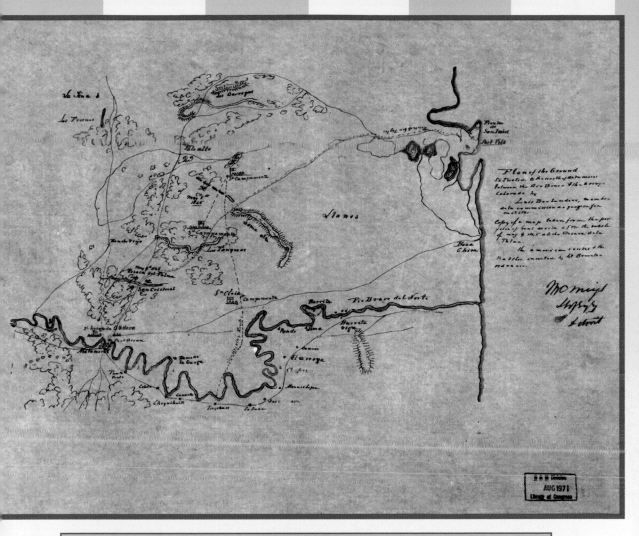

This map shows the American routes during the campaign that resulted in the capture of Colonel Fannin's troops.

Este mapa muestra las rutas seguidas por los norteamericanos y que condujeron a la captura de las tropas del coronel Fannin.

2 THE TEXAS REVOLUTION

At this time in history, Texas was fighting for independence from Mexico. Texas was not yet part of the United States. The colonists of Texas wished to set up their own republic. But Mexico wanted control of Texas. It was a very bloody war, but eventually the colonists of Texas won their revolution.

2 LA REVOLUCIÓN TEXANA

En este momento de la historia, Texas aún no era parte de Estados Unidos y luchaba por independizarse de México. Los colonos de Texas deseaban establecer su propia república, pero México quería el control del territorio. Fue una guerra muy sangrienta, pero al final triunfó la revolución de los colonos.

The Battle of San Jacinto, April 1836. The Texans defeated Santa Anna's troops, and with this victory they secured their independence.

La Batalla de San Jacinto, abril de 1836. Los texanos derrotaron a las tropas de Santa Anna y aseguraron su independencia.

The Goliad Massacre is one of the most famous events of the Texas Revolution. General Antonio López de Santa Anna asked for and received a decree from the Mexican Congress that all foreigners bearing arms against Mexico and taken as prisoners should be shot.

———◆◆◆———

La Masacre de Goliad es uno de los acontecimientos más famosos de la Revolución Texana. El general Antonio López de Santa Anna pidió al Congreso mexicano que aprobara un decreto según el cual todos los extranjeros que se alzaran contra México y fueran tomados prisioneros, deberían ser pasados por las armas. Este decreto fue aprobado.

UNANIMOUS

DECLARATION OF INDEPENDENCE,

BY THE

DELEGATES OF THE PEOPLE OF TEXAS,

IN GENERAL CONVENTION,

AT THE TOWN OF WASHINGTON,

ON THE SECOND DAY OF MARCH, 1836.

RICHARD ELLIS, *President.*

The Texas Declaration of Independence, adopted on March 2, 1836, declared Texas a free and independent republic.

La Declaración de Independencia de Texas que data del 2 de marzo de 1836, declaraba a Texas una república libre e independiente.

After losing the Battle of Coleto Creek, Texas colonel James W. Fannin and his troops were out of food, water, and ammunition. They had no choice but to surrender to Mexican forces. General José de Urrea stated that Fannin and his men would be treated in a civilized manner as prisoners of war.

Después de perder la batalla de Coleto Creek, al coronel texano James W. Fannin y a sus tropas se les habían acabado los alimentos, el agua y las municiones. No tenían más remedio que rendirse a las fuerzas mexicanas. El general José de Urrea aseguró que Fannin y sus hombres iban a ser tratados de manera civilizada como prisioneros de guerra.

COSTUMES MEXICAINS.

Dragon. Troupe de Ligne.

A Mexican dragoon, a cavalry officer

Un dragón mexicano u oficial de caballería

17

Fannin and his troops, more than 300 men, gave up their weapons and surrendered. When General Santa Anna heard about the agreement between Urrea and Fannin, he ordered that Urrea follow the decree of the Mexican Congress and shoot Fannin's troops.

Fannin y sus tropas, más de 300 hombres, entregaron sus armas y se rindieron. Cuando el general Santa Anna se enteró del acuerdo entre Urrea y Fannin, ordenó que se obedeciera el decreto del Congreso mexicano y pasara por las armas a las tropas de Fannin.

James Walker Fannin Jr., commander of the men massacred at Goliad

James Walker Fannin Jr., comandante de los hombres masacrados en Goliad

3 THE ANGEL OF GOLIAD

When Francisca arrived at Goliad with Captain Alvarez, the Texan rebels had just been taken prisoner. The men's wrists had been tightly bound with cords. They had been forced to stand this way for hours, without water or food. Francisca's heart went out to them.

3 EL ÁNGEL DE GOLIAD

Cuando Francisca llegó a Goliad con el capitán Alvarez, los rebeldes texanos habían caido prisioneros. Les habían atado las muñecas con cuerdas muy apretadas. Les habían obligado a estar de pie durante horas, sin agua ni alimentos. El corazón de Francisca se apiadó de ellos.

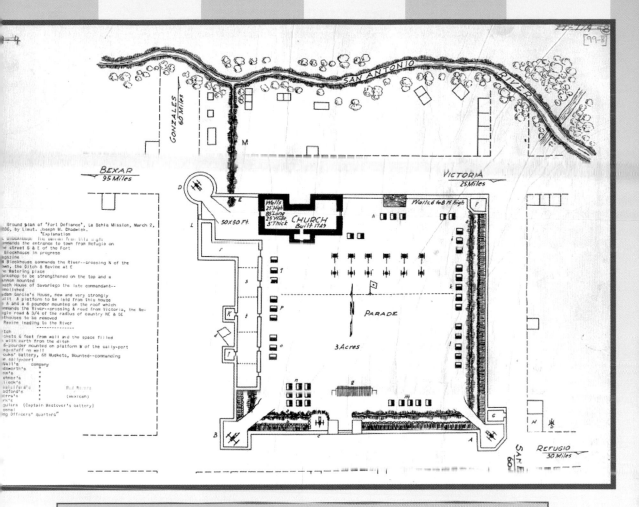

Mission La Bahia, where the Texans were taken after their defeat

Misión La Bahía, donde fueron llevados los texanos después de la derrota

Francisca had the cords removed from the men's wrists. She made sure that they had something to drink. She treated them with kindness when no one else would. The next morning, Francisca discovered that the men were to be killed. She pleaded with military officers until they agreed to spare the lives of twenty doctors, interpreters, nurses, and mechanics.

———————— ◆◆◆ ————————

Francisca hizo que les quitaran las cuerdas que ataban sus muñecas. Se aseguró de que les dieran algo de beber. Los trató con bondad cuando nadie lo hizo. A la mañana siguiente, Francisca supo que los iban a matar. Rogó a los oficiales del ejercito que les perdonaran la vida a veinte doctores, intérpretes, enfermeros y mecánicos.

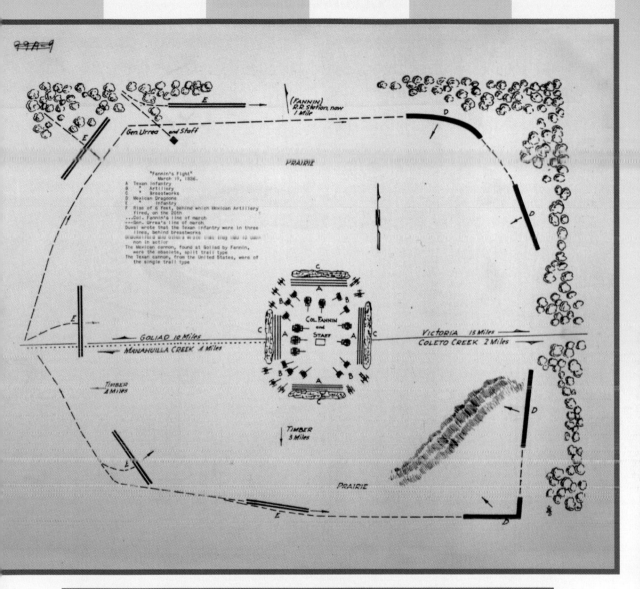

A sketch of the fortifications Colonel Fannin established at the Battle of Coleto Creek before surrender

Un boceto de las fortificaciones que el coronel Fannin estableció en la batalla de Coleto Creek, antes de rendirse

On the morning of March 27, 1836, the prisoners were marched out of town. At a certain spot along the way, the group was stopped. The guards fired at the prisoners at close range. Most were killed right away. Those who were not killed were pursued and slaughtered.

En la mañana del 27 de marzo de 1836, los prisioneros fueron obligados a marchar fuera del pueblo. En un punto del camino, el grupo se detuvo. Los guardias dispararon a los prisioneros a quemarropa. Casi todos murieron enseguida. A los que no murieron, los persiguieron y los mataron a sangre fría.

[Domestic Correspondence]

Statement of J. C. Duval.

Genl Santa Anna and Genl Urrea also
I have understood, after their return to
Mexico, in order to palliate their in
human butchery of four hundred un-
armed prisoners at Goliad, asserted
" that Col Fannin and his men had
Surrendered "unconditionally."

(TX) I will state as briefly as possible
and to the best of my recollection, what
occurred the morning after the battle
at the Coletto creek.

The morning after the battle of
Coletto creek, Col Fannin and his men
were Surrounded on the open prairie
by an overwhelming force of the enemy
They had formed their line of battle, and
fired several rounds of grape and can-
nister from their artillery at our en-

The statement by John C. Duval, one of the survivors of the massacre

La declaración de John C. Duval, uno de los sobrevivientes de la masacre

25

Francisca also concealed several more prisoners until the shooting was over. The Texans were so grateful to her that they named her the Angel of Goliad.

After the Goliad Massacre, Francisca returned to Mexico City with Captain Alvarez. He then deserted her, leaving her penniless. After Alvarez left her, Francisca was never heard of again.

Francisca también escondió algunos otros prisioneros hasta que terminó el tiroteo. Los tejanos estaban tan agradecidos que la llamaron el Ángel de Goliad.

Después de la Masacre de Goliad, Francisca volvió a Ciudad México con el capitán Alvarez. Este la abandonó dejándola sin un centavo. Nunca más se oyó hablar de ella.

Bust of Francisca Alvarez located at Presidio La Bahia

Busto de Francisca Alvarez en Presidio La Bahía

27

Francisca Alvarez felt that people should not suffer or be treated unfairly, no matter what side they were on.

The men killed at Goliad have memorials in Texas dedicated to their memory. Although there isn't a memorial to Francisca, the Angel of Goliad, she will always be remembered for her kindness and courage.

Francisca Alvarez pensaba que la gente no debía sufrir o ser tratada injustamente, sin importar a qué bando perteneciera.

En Texas existen monumentos dedicados a los hombres asesinados en Goliad. Aunque no exista un monumento a Francisca, el Ángel de Goliad, ella siempre será recordada por su bondad y valentía.

The survivors of the Goliad Massacre

Los sobrevivientes de la Masacre de Goliad

29

TIMELINE

1834–1835—Francisca Alvarez becomes the common-law wife of Captain Telesforo Alvarez.

March 26, 1836—Francisca Alvarez discovers the mistreatment of the prisoners of war. She has them untied and fed.

April 21, 1836—The Texas Revolution ends with the Battle of San Jacinto.

October 1835—The Texas Revolution begins at the Battle of Gonzales.

March 27, 1836—The Goliad Massacre. More than 300 Texans are shot to death by the Mexican army. More than 20 Texans are saved because of the efforts of Francisca Alvarez.

CRONOLOGÍA

1834–1835—Francisca Alvarez se convierte en la compañera del capitán Telesforo Alvarez

26 de marzo 1836—Francisca Alvarez descubre el maltrato a los prisioneros de guerra. Los hace desatar y alimentar.

21 de abril, 1836—Termina la Revolución Texana con la batalla de San Jacinto.

Octubre de 1835—Comienza la Revolución Texana con la batalla de Gonzales.

27 de marzo, 1836—La Masacre de Goliad. Más de 300 texanos son pasados por las armas por el ejército mexicano. Se salvan más de 20 gracias a los esfuerzos de Francisca Alvarez.

GLOSSARY

decree (dih-KREE) An official order.

interpreter (in-TER-prih-ter) Someone who translates the meanings of words from one language to another.

massacre (MAH-sih-ker) When many people are killed at one time.

memorial (meh-MOR-ee-uhl) A statute or structure established in memory of a person or group of people.

rebel (REH-bul) A person who fights against authority.

revolution (reh-vuh-LOO-shun) When people decide to overthrow a government.

WEB SITES

Due to the changing nature of Internet links, the Rosen Publishing Group, Inc., has developed an online list of Web sites related to the subject of this book. This site is updated regularly. Please use this link to access the list:

http://www.rosenlinks.com/fpah/falv

GLOSARIO

decreto (el) Una orden oficial.

intérprete (el, la) Alguien que traduce los significados de las palabras de una lengua a otra.

masacre (la) Cuando matan a mucha gente al mismo tiempo.

monumento (el) Una estatua o estructura dedicada a la memoria de una persona o de un grupo de personas.

pasar por las armas Ejecutar a una persona o soldado enemigo.

rebelde (el, la) Una persona que lucha contra la autoridad.

revolución (la) Cuando la gente decide derrocar un gobierno.

SITOS WEB

Debido a las constantes modificaciones en los sitios de Internet, Rosen Publishing Group, Inc., ha desarrollado un listado de sitios Web relacionados con el tema de este libro. Este sitio se actualiza con regularidad. Por favor, usa este enlace para acceder a la lista:

http://www.rosenlinks.com/fpah/falv

INDEX

ABOUT THE AUTHOR

Tracie Egan is a freelance writer who lives in New York City.

ÍNDICE

ACERCA DEL AUTOR

Tracie Egan es escritora independiente. Vive en la ciudad de Nueva York.